UNMARKED DOORS

ALSO BY INGE ISRAEL

Réflexions
     (Editions Saint Germain-des-Prés: Paris, 1978)

Même le soleil a des taches
     (Editions Saint Germain-des-Prés: Paris, 1980)

Aux quatre terres
     (Les Editions du Vermillon: Ottawa, 1990)

Raking Zen Furrows: Encounters with Japan
     (Cacanadadada Press: Vancouver, 1991)

UNMARKED DOORS

Poems
by

Inge Israel

CACANADADADA

UNMARKED DOORS
Copyright © 1992 Inge Israel

Published by

CACANADADADA PRESS LTD.
3350 West 21st Avenue
Vancouver, B.C. Canada
V6S 1G7

Set in Baskerville 11 pt on 13½
Typesetting: The Typeworks, Vancouver, B.C.
Printing: Hignell Printing, Winnipeg, Manitoba
Cover Design: Cecilia Jang
Cover Art: Alvin Jang

Canadian Cataloguing in Publication Data

Israel, Inge.
    Unmarked doors

    ISBN 0-921870-16-7

    I. Title.
PS8567.S73U5 1992   C811'.54   C92-091410-1
PR9199.3.I87U5 1992

To Werner with love

ACKNOWLEDGEMENTS

With affection and gratitude to Ronald B. Hatch and to my family and friends for their wonderful interest and encouragement.

The author gratefully acknowledges the support of the Alberta Foundation for the Arts.

Poems in this collection have appeared in the following magazines: *Quarry, Canadian Ethnic Studies, Physics in Canada, Garm Lu, Prairie Fire, White Wall Review, Northward Journal, On Spec, Poets' Gallery, Implosion.*

Three of the poems are re-workings of pieces originally published in French in the author's *Aux quatre terres*.

Some poems from the sequence "Whirl is King" were read at the Edmonton Space and Science Centre.

"Northern Journey" was broadcast by the CBC, then set to music for baritone and piano by Canadian Composer Violet Archer and premiered in 1991 at the University of Alberta.

"Clean Breast" forms the basis of a radio drama commissioned by the CBC, as well as a play to be staged in the near future.

"Russian Diary" is shortly to be broadcast on the CBC.

Contents

"The cosmos is about the smallest hole
a man can hide his head in."
— G.K. CHESTERTON

PROLOGUE

CAPE SPEAR
Newfoundland

Icebergs, phantom chariots,
glide by   aloof
while Atlantic surf pounds
fingers of land
that claw
toward Europe
millions of years
and a world of thought away
yet near as the glint in an eye

the rock
redreaming the parting,
raises tips of red jackets,
miniature torches
pointing the way.

CLEAN BREAST

Nora Barnacle Joyce—a confession

CLEAN BREAST

Bless me Father . . .
ah I've lost the words
I can hardly say them now
In the convent school
I had them off by heart
Now   after all these years
with Jim   my mouth has a mind
of its own   so it's hard to say
Bless me Father for I have sinned

Thirty-seven years we lived
together   with Jim never able
to make himself go into a church
not even to get married   putting
a ring on his own finger
just to ward off blindness
and letting me buy one for myself
Oh I know right enough what's
in his books   I'm bound to
Wasn't he sixteen years planning
Ulysses   seven writing it
and all the while talking about
nothing else   Many's the time
God would have made his tongue rot
in his mouth   if He weren't
all-merciful and able to read
Jim's mind   and see there was no evil
in it   only this roaring appetite
for words   for bits and pieces
about everything   that he chewed up

So much shit   I'm sorry Father
so much dung inside one person
no wonder it came tumbling out
of him again like chop suey
every bit of it with more than one
meaning

Isn't it well for the people
who see only the clever side
the trouble is
my words are in his books too

"I'm like a pebble in your hands   Nora
everything deep and true and moving
in what I write comes from you"   he said
thinking it would please me to hear it
but it's a terrible weight

I know Father   it was wrong
to leave Ireland with him
in the first place   and I only
a green slip of a Galway girl
working as a maid at Finn's Hotel
alone in Dublin   then going off
with a man who wouldn't marry me
telling no-one
Jim able to talk the moon
into taking a new path in the sky
but he had a true regard for me
and the face of a saint on him
I'm not trying to find excuses
the thought of going to Paris
had me mad with love for him
and I've stuck with him
all these years

I wouldn't give a snap of my fingers
for a man that hasn't a bit of the devil
in him   But *read* that book
how could I   and it full of all
the dirt in the world   everything
dirty the same for him as cowdung
for flies   that he'd shape into puns
and string out as if they were grapes
on God's own vine   "Nora"   he'd say
"*Ulysses* is like the Bible   a book
no good Catholic should read
but if it's not fit to read
life isn't fit to live
There's good mixed with bad in all
things"   he'd say   "and in *Ulysses*
all I've done is record every
single thought and sensation
a human being has in the course
of one day"   "Well Jim"   I'd say
"that's not art   you might as well
copy out the London Directory"
"That's not how it is at all"
he'd say   "it's like a mountain
that I tunnel into from every
direction   not knowing what
I'll find when I get inside
the way I do with you Nora"

I'm sorry Father   that's what he said
and doesn't God mean men to do that
or why are we made that way
Isn't everything His invention

No I never read *Ulysses* though
Jim gave me a copy the way a cat
would lay a dead mouse at your feet
expecting you to eat it

9

"Das Buch ist ein Schwein"
I told him   but he couldn't
make himself see it from outside

I learned the signposts of his mind
the way a postman learns the bends
and turns of the lanes and alleys
he'd go through   "Jim"   I'd say
"why don't you give up writing
and take up singing"
such a fine singing voice   he had
even getting the Bronze Medal
for tenor in the *Feis Ceoil* once

but he was a squid   with language
for ink   not squirting a single
thing straight   his heart maddened
with delight at every twist
he could add   even sitting
with a suitcase on his lap
to write on   and us like two
God-forsaken gypsies by the roadside
forever on the move   forever trying
to find new lodgings
like the Holy Family
in Trieste   in Rome   in Zürich   in Paris
trying to scrape together the rent
before we'd be kicked out again
some of the places not fit
to wash a rat in   me taking in
washing to help out   "laundress"
it said on my papers

There were times I was that lonesome
I'd weep for days
for Ireland   for my children

never seeing their cousins or aunts
or grandparents   under a sun
rising on mornings without a name
and strange alien birds in the sky
the town often so thronged
and warm   it would train you for hell
wishing I was married to a man
like my father   instead of living
with a weakling who'd faint
at the sight of a rat for fear
it would bring him bad luck
so afraid of a fist   he wasn't able
to describe a fight in his own books
a man who'd dive under the table
in a thunderstorm   who put his head
under my skirts
not only for the one reason
but the way an ostrich would in sand
living in this world and not living
in it at all   sniffing out
the real truth   till an overdose
of it would send him scurrying off
into his jungle of words by way
of a retreat

When I told Hemingway   "Jim could do
with a spot of that lion-hunting"
just the mention of it
terrified him   "I wouldn't be able
to see the lion with my bad eyes"
he said   "Never mind Jim"   I told him
"Hemingway'd describe him to you
and afterwards you could go up
and touch him   and smell him
that's all you ever need
to write into your books"

11

I loved him   Father   weak as he was
The Lord have mercy on his soul

though at times I wanted to take
the children and run to some quiet place
of my own   away from his drinking
and wandering   and always being paupers

But Jim had a great mind
oh the way that man could explain
how sound is only there   if you hear it
and colour   if you see it
and a shape   if you can touch it
A smell in his nose was enough
to kindle a fire in his head   he could
build a whole world into a fart
I'm sorry Father   wind   but he never
used a dirty word in front of a lady
nor did he like other men to do it
either   he was a real gentleman
though when it came to drink
he'd be strong-willed as a mule
and with the terrible thirst
of a man mounting rocks

Oh the nights he'd be drinking
with his cronies   wiping the hours
off the clock with their jabbering
till time lay dead in the empty
streets   and someone would push
him into a taxi for home
the driver bringing him to the door
bedraggled   his hat crooked
on his head   for me to put to bed

the way you would a child
him trying to break away from me
to go skipping down the road
shouting   "Free free   at last"
saying drinking came as easy
to him as scolding to a woman
even trying to climb a lamp-post
one Saint Patrick's night
"Faith   I tell you   I'll have
the children baptized to-morrow"
I'd say   to bring him to his senses
when he'd start on one of his bouts

You see Father   he needed me

I saw them in the bars
where they'd spend their nights
with girls collecting round
their table   some of them big
draught horses of girls
prancing about   shameless
like mares in heat   and Jim
with his head back   tasting
every dirty word that would fall
off their tongues as if they were
apples in the Garden of Eden
I had to do what I could
to keep him away from them
so I'd drag him home and warm
his poor prick   sorry Father
in my hands   and I'd try
to be the men and women he dreamed
about with no clothes on
even when I couldn't stand him
touching me at all   till it felt
like a terrible punishment

13

It was the same with the letters
I wrote him   Father   when we
weren't together   oh I know
they were sinful   but wasn't it
better for me to write them
so he could get his rise
from my words   than have him go
chasing some whore   wouldn't
any woman do the same   God has
some nature in Him   so maybe
with a little help from you
Father   He'll understand

Some nights   Jim would say
he was a beast   eating like a beast
lusting like a beast   dying like a beast
but he'd always been dreaming
of a PURE love   maybe that's why
he thought the world of Dante
who never touched his Beatrice
they say   but how can they be sure

Here I am   talking only about Jim
and it's my confession   The trouble
is   after 37 years   I don't know
what's him and what's me
even with him gone

Would you be able to put in a word
for him too in your prayers   Father
though what he'd say if he heard me
with you now   will   from this day on
be a salmon leaping in my breast

but I couldn't   let them give him
a catholic burial   I couldn't
do that to him though it was
a terrible sin to say no

just thinking of it was enough
to put his nightmare in my head
till I'd hear him calling out to me
"A starry snake has kissed me
a cold nightsnake   Noraah"

I don't know   was it crawling
round his sister when they were
small   calling her Eve   pretending
he was the serpent   had him that way
or was it another boy at Clongowes
College pushing him into the cesspool
till he was sick with fever
marked him for life
"I'm just lowering a bucket down to
my soul's well"   he'd say
"and the memories I draw up   I put
into my writing"   But I wonder Father
was it memories he had by the tail
or only his imagination
indeed there were times it was
every bit like a sickness

Puns would keep that man laughing
in a town with plague

"Books should express the holy spirit
of joy"   he'd say   "my name is my omen
Nora"   and the next minute he'd call
himself James Joyless
his moods chancy as a Galway day

and want me to rip off his trousers
and flog him like a naughty schoolboy

With *Finnegans Wake* he'd sit up
nights laughing that hard   it would
stop a carthorse from sleeping
letting words lead him to things
not things to words

Sometimes   drunk into a trance
his blue eyes big as a cow's
he'd be sitting in one of those bars
in the middle of all the noise
the clink of glasses   jazz music
the chatter and giggling of whores
and be reciting long pieces of Dante
in Italian   the way a priest
would say Mass   Oh he had
the makings of a priest   wasn't he
always thinking about immortality
only not the way a man of God
would   Jim thought he could get it
with his books   if he stuck enough
puzzles and tricks and code words
in where they'd be hard to find
so people would never forget him
but go on forever digging   the way
dogs would dig out bones   worrying
them   licking them   maybe hiding
them again so they could start
over another day   And isn't it
the truth   they DO go on reading
his books   and talking about him

16

You see   Father   he put everything
in those books   the worst sins
you could imagine   and wouldn't you
call that a kind of confession
for it's more than ordinary people
read them   I've seen priests
at it too   and I know there are
question and answer parts
with meanings only astronomers
or scientists could make head or tail of

He said   "I'm writing it all down
to show how extraordinary
ordinary people are
and when I write"   he said
"I perform a natural function
just as a tree produces fruit"

In the eyes of the world   Jim started
off a bad boy and ended up an old
codger   But tell me   Father
is anyone truly good

Mad keen he was   to break down
barriers and be the great liberator
but wasn't he the captive himself
in the end   not able to flick
his little finger but there'd be
an outcry   some people for him
but many more against
even the Marxists attacking him
though he said nobody in his books
was worth more than £1000

Egoarch   he'd call Ibsen
though he thought the world of him
it was always Ibsen this and Ibsen
that   till I used to wonder did he
only want me for my name being
the same as Ibsen used in a play
Once he gave away a good £10 note
to Shelley's grandniece   for her
name was Nora   I used to wonder too
did we only leave Ireland because
Ibsen left his country   Jim was
always looking for coincidences
saying they're sacred
but I know he made some of them
happen himself   The time he said
he felt Barnacled and wanted to leave
me   was when he heard a rumour
about Ibsen leaving his wife

But he had a Big Bertha of an ego
himself   did my Jim   not the scrappy
little firecrackers that fizzled
around him   the full-blown ego
of a full-blown genius   no taste
only genius   you could tell
even when he was dumb as an oyster
he'd still look clever
He wouldn't give Freud the time of day
but people say he was just like him
the two of them uncovering what had
always been out of sight
Wasn't it funny Jim's
name meaning joy   the same as Freud's

Now there's a man who disturbed
the sleep of the world   It must have
been hard on Mrs Freud too
they say he had another woman
his sister-in-law   the three of them
living under the same roof

When Jim wanted me to go with other men
it was as if he'd stuck a knife in me
Oh I know   it was only to fire himself
up with jealousy   so he'd have more
ideas to put in his books
In the strange workings of his mind
it was a way of proving his regard
for me   His books had him blinder
than the sickness in his eyes   It wasn't easy
always chasing after his tail   or trying
to unravel what he was saying to me

but we belonged together   Father

He didn't only call me his fuckbird
sorry Father   his portable Ireland
he said I was   his home away from home
he'd never hurt a fly   a good man he was
and a good father   always thinking
of the children   it's not many
men you can say that of
and that generous   nothing was
ever too dear or too good
if it was for me or the children

19

At times   drunk   he'd weep
telling of the large family
he was from   all of them with
twelve or eighteen children
and he'd swear by the grace of God
he'd have as many himself   but two
was more than I could manage
traipsing around all over the world
with never a proper home

and poor Lucia not right in her
head   and to top it all   much too
fond of Jim   falling right in
that trap the devil sets
between a girl and her father
oh he never took advantage of her
though it's a temptation must be
on many a father's mind

It wasn't only Jim she was too fond of
there was her brother too   mad
with jealousy she was when he got
married   and then there was Beckett

God knows Jim moved mountains
doing his best for her   never
letting himself believe she was
that far gone   refusing to get
her certified   "She's no madder
than her father"   he said
even when they had to carry her out
in a straight-jacket   It hurt him
too much   you see   and it's true
enough there's often more sense
in mad people than the wise
but living with them takes more
strength than a plain mortal
would have

20

and all the while   Jim losing
his sight   my heart would break
watching him grope his way down
the stairs   like a cathedral spire
going down in a storm

and I'd ask myself   did God send
all those misfortunes to correct me
or was it the devil   tempting me
People would say   "Nora's SO funny
all that Irish wit and humour"

and Jim thought I was the strong one
but God knows   I was often
that tormented I'd be the blind man
leading the blind

like the times he fell in love
and I never let on I knew

He said   if I'd only read the books
he gave me   we'd be able to speak together
But others had no trouble speaking
to me   He said for me to wear
tight naughty blouses   and frilly drawers
with great crimson bows on them
heavy with perfume
But others didn't need those things
to be fond of me
Oh I had admirers
And there was one . . .
Yes
There was one

But all that's past now

Many's the time I'd have
a powerful wish   to make my own book
If Jim could put down my words
why couldn't I do the same
My dreams he put down too
making me tell him all I could remember

But I was never much of a writer
my hands were full   minding one
who worked on his lines
the way a fighter with true red
blood in him would fight
going altogether wild
A Champion   who made all
the world into Joyce country

We had a long while together
coming and going   stopping
and learning strange tongues
then moving on again
from place to place

yes   a long while   before
the night with no arms to rest in

still it was sudden
him closing his eyes   taking my words
with him beyond the grave
leaving me on the edge
of emptiness   deep as the sea
his voice a restless wave

Jim   Jim
I'm not turning my back on you
You're safe under my skirts

but it's me I'm thinking of now

Mother of God   pray for me

RUSSIAN DIARY

MOSCOW WATERWAYS

Each spring, watching
the Saskatchewan break up, I tried
to imagine these other far-away
rivers I now see before me.

They flowed over clutching roots
through tales my mother told me.
Through her eyes I saw
the sparkling ice blocks,
in her voice I heard their cracks
and muffled clinks and chinks
as they stubbed one another
on their way to freedom,
sounds nostalgic as the liquid
phrase of a balalaika. . . .

Subterranean rivers abound
in Moscow; the map does not trace
their paths but in the depths
the water tunnels
dark over muddy memories
to a sea
both beginning and end.

NIGHT TRAIN TO LENINGRAD

Here, near these legendary steppes,
the sky's height sharpens
no perspective,
only breadth and continuity overwhelm.

Time is outwitted. Moments of far ago
burst into sudden clarity:
my father, a teenager,
his tousled head among the others
he drew so carefully
in the internment camp,
lining up for their soup, working
the waterwheel and, in the sketch
he called "The Hunt"—a rare touch
of humour—they sit on the ground
delousing themselves.

All eight sketches hang on my wall
at home. I've watched them fade
over the years, pleaded for help
at museums, at galleries. "No!"
I was told, "Unethical to touch."
Unethical? To stop this slow
second death? Desperate,
using a pen and special ink,
I went over even the tiniest leaf,
recognizing my father in every loop,
following his lead
as I had never done in life
and now, on this train
where I've pushed aside the curtain
and the curtain under that

then prised open the blind,
he guides me still
to feel the thrust of a roof beam,
the tilt of a head,
the crook of an arm.

CATHERINE PALACE

Up marble stairs
under crystal chandeliers
and gold-leaf everywhere
we shuffle along in large
felt slippers, as out of place
as the first peasants
who crossed these thresholds
blinded
by the aristocrats' glitter

as out of place as you,
little mother, would have felt
had you lived to return here.

Your quaking presence fills
a vacuum beside me as I pad
across these precious inlaid
floors once trod
by Catherine the Great
and the husband
she imprisoned;
the same Catherine
whose little finger
more than a century later
was carried, embalmed,
at the head of processions
followed by throngs of people
squabbling to be closest
to the front,
closest to the cherished finger
and you, a small girl
straining to see,

asking "What's so special
about a finger?" before
you found out about fingers
and hands and salutes.

I pad across these splendid floors
amidst other throngs, all of us
shod in silent felt slippers
which do not fit and we pull them
this way and that,
tie and retie them
and still they hang askew
on our uncomprehending feet.

GLASNOST, *Moscow*

On Arbat Street,
newly closed to traffic,
artists sit by their easels
—tentative buds
of free enterprise.

In the Church
mostly old women gather,
their attention held
not by the priest
nor the service
but by a longing
in the stained glass.
Glass is a slow liquid
its tears slower
than man's dust.
All longing is the same.

The guide, her strong voice
rising above the priest's,
explains in numbing detail
architecture and history.
Twice he asks her
to take us elsewhere or, at least,
not disturb the service.
She pretends deafness.

An old woman seated on a bench
looks at me
and I at her.

Without words we speak
about this toothless soil
god-breeding and god-devouring.

Once I saw a butterfly
perched on a turtle's head
drinking salt from a tear
in the corner of the turtle's eye.
All thirst is the same.

RETURN FLIGHT

We nose our way up, the tail
hanging low as if weighed down
by the desperate crowds we saw
in grim queues
while English students seated
at the back, sing "Moscow Nights"
with Slav melancholy.

Below us, the "Aurora" lies
at anchor, a slowly diminishing relic
of the '17 Uprising,
its promise unfulfilled.

More speed now
and the trail of smoke
from our BOA jet
is linear elation.

Drinks start to flow and suddenly
we're over Riga—"Yay, Riga!"
shout the students.
Trays are passed round: real kiwi!
Strawberries! Fresh vegetables!
But only on this side of clouds
bright as Leningrad White Nights.

Eight o'clock now, we're crossing
the border. "Yay, the BORDER!"
they shout. But the figure-eight
is a Möbius strip offering no escape
and the sun's reflection
in the 'plane's wing, a Moscow Cupola.

THE COURSE

THE COURSE

At first it is a groan
a deep   A A A A *A*
                        A

that falls off
the line, down the page
and splinters on the floor.

> For a whole week
> a robin hops
> on the window sill.
> The decision is not easy.

Be savage, gentle, anything.
One word will force the next,
dredge up forgotten events,
buried traumas. Five pages
a day, at least.

> The woods look candid,
> the world proportioned,
> the moment ripe,
> inveigling the robin to build,
> twig by painstaking twig,
> blind to the lines, scars,
> codes on the bark.

Some of us skirt edges,
write songs; others wade
across sands of inner
landscapes (can anything grow in sand?
        sand flea, sand fly, sand worm . . .)

We hand in our five, ten
even thirty pages.

What of the people
we willy-nilly expose
by our own nudity?
Have no scruples: given shape,
disloyalties and anomalies
become art.

       The robin's heart is
       in her nest, now complete
       on the window sill.
       In full view. Silly bird!
       She has laid three eggs
       speckled, fragile.

What if something does grow,
strains toward the sun,
sending down roots
never to be dislodged?

What if one of us births
a monster never to be
disowned?
Have no scruples: given shape,
disloyalties and anomalies
become art.

I tell him about the eggs,
how I check daily.
He comes.
We look at them together, rapt,
growing heartbeat of syllables.

Not far away, a deer loses
its footing, falls down
a steep slope, drags itself
to a hiding place
to die or recover.
Does it know which?
Here, even death could look
harmless.

We discover it can be done,
one consonant at a time
like raindrops finding their way
underground.

Outside the window, the canvas
fills with faces,
familiar profiles in the eaves,
eyes, chins on branches.
And there, tears
roll down a green cheek, unguarded.
And mouths everywhere!
Open, closed, speaking, speaking. . . .

At night, the instructors
carry off the sheaves of paper,
examine them under light;
by day, we discuss their findings.
It's summer,
two wear white
shirts and pants.

It cannot be ignored:
even in this valley, among these
fragrant pines, they're the doctors
or nurses at the Sanatorium
on their way to the lab,

carrying jars
containing our specimens
the sputum we coughed up
often painfully and saved,
trembling, to be tested
for reality—traces of blood
or living bacilli.

At the San
it was Georgia's third year
and my third week. "Baby", she said,
"you hasn't even warmed the bed yet!
But don't you worry, honey,
sickly folks never dies.
They just hangs around
and stays sick."

As a cheery reminder
that we were all
in the same boat,
privacy was forbidden.
Through wide doors,
the months dripped, acid
on raw nerves.
Gaps between endless waits
for lab results were filled
with despair, books, visitors
—mostly reluctant passengers
who stepped aboard briefly,
afraid to touch anything,
afraid to breathe.
Apologetic, we couldn't stop exhaling
tainted molecules of air.
Though Carol did, a thin wisp
of a girl who made a flowered dress
to wear in summer,
but died in spring.

Not only are we getting better
acquainted,
everyone is growing more
purposeful, as if the equator
were receding, the pull
of gravity more intense.

"Honey, I'm just as happy as a lark
singing on the fence in the springtime!"
Georgia beamed. "They're gonna let me
go two times a week, over to that there
school, so the students can paint my
face. Artistic leave, is what it is!"

He goes climbing for the weekend.
We are aeons apart.
I go to bed remembering the deer
and my ankle hurts in my sleep.

Is the rockslide triggered
by my dream? He very nearly does not
escape.
To think a pebble
might have extinguished all!

I walk along the riverbank
and, with his deep fear of water,
see two lovers embrace
on a steep, narrow path
above the churning eddies.

The robin's eggs have hatched;
she clearly wishes her feathers
were still scales and her brood
far from this high noon
of evolution.
But safe?...

During a coffee-break, something snaps.
After nights of being "savage, gentle,
anything," of "dredging up forgotten
traumas," Jan throws the coffee-maker
at one of the instructors.

> "Don't you trust them doctors,
> and nurses, baby!" Georgia said.

Eyes are showing strain
and cheeks pallor;
urgency has crept in
through the cracks.
The world beyond the woods is
a receding galaxy
while we flit about
and learn
the radar skill of bats.

> Shirley had lain
> on her stomach a full year,
> not allowed to turn.
> Her symptoms were classical
> but no living organisms
> ever showed in her tests.
> Was this why she managed to laugh
> even on the day her husband said
> he was leaving her for someone else?

But once, when a starlit sky
was framed in the window,
she broke down and wept.
It was Saturday night
—she wanted to "do the town."
Maria, a pro, was quick:
"Go on! On a Saturday? It's the most
vulgar night of the week!" she laughed.
And death? Isn't it vulgar?

There is a tightening
in the gyre: massive regions
shrinking toward points
of density . . . and the wily moon
poses as a safety net!

Fingers pound typewriters furiously.
All day I hear his
now see him in the dark,
the definition imprecise,
his outline entangled
in black shadows.

In the morning, still sensing
the depths, he cries at the sound
of his own words,
at the sound of mine.

In the morning,
a woodpecker paraphrases
primal drumming.
Perched at my height,
he is fearless as I pass.

The air fills with danger,
spaces beween lines
wait to suck in
treading feet.

        The baby robins are all beak
        wide open, trusting.

He has made a drawing of them
in their nest
and gives it to me. In case . . .

        At the San
        do-gooders, suppressing their fear,
        wallowing in virtue,
        came to earn their brownie points
        sitting by our beds,
        taunting fate.
        But no George Sand among them
        to kiss a consumptive Chopin
        squarely on the mouth.

        Hands folded in her lap,
        ankles and knees together, prim,
        one asked me, "Is it true
        that TB increases
        the—ahem—libido?"
        Furious, speechless,
        I wished for Georgia's ease,
        "Yes ma'mam, hottest stuff ever was,
        nothing but fucking on our minds!"

The present is a cloven hoof;
its double gallop echoes
in the woods. Incestuous
longings uncoil, reptilian
from the branches
and fruit dangles, misshapen.

The water looks innocent,
pure, but is not.
Kettles boil, even for brushing
teeth. But the juice machine's
connection to the tap is overlooked.
They find me on the floor
in the middle of the night. I cannot
rise, their voices and silhouettes
merge dizzily above me, their faces
lilies opening and closing.

At the hospital, galvanized
by my dwindling pulse, the nurse says,
"I can't get a doctor,
Would you like a priest?"
She shrinks back at my smile.

Whose blood are they pumping
into me? (suspended above the bed,
it invades my body drop by viscid drop)
Whose wishes are now tugging
this and that way
in my veins?
Disconnect it! Hurry! PLEASE!
I must leave.
The course is ending.

The first time
I briefly left the San,
rebirth overwhelmed me.
Blades of grass jutted, momentous.
I stroked them
singly as if coaxing tendrils
to lean on me, though it was I
who leaned.

Trees brought a lump to my throat.
I fingered their bark,
its living roughness,
every existing thing miraculous
compared to nothingness.

The first time
I left the San
each moment was a postponement.

I am back
and, in the early dawn
run to the nest.

He is there.
It is empty.
Our eyes meet.
Two feathers rise from the ground,
float away.

ALBUM

OVER THE PRAIRIE

I saw a cloud
and stared in disbelief:
Mozart in profile.

Shifting imperceptibly,
a frown spread over the brow,
features thickened.
The chiseled nose
coarsened, the mouth turned
into a firm chin,
the wig uncurled

the mood darkened

into a Beethoven cloudburst.

HIDING ANGLES
for Douglas Cardinal, architect.

Once I was whole.
Once when language was more than a cry
a wild flower whispered worlds,
all things had a melody
even the rock.

I woo heavens with my cathedrals,
hide angles in rounded shapes
but they are made of others' stones.
I lift my voice in prayer
but the words are not mine.

Freezing skies bite
stones and words
indifferent suns burn them,
disperse them forever
in heartless space.

I bend low
searching Blackfoot roots.

ELM TREE
for Elizabeth Smart

Dusk on Bloor Street still stirs the guilt
I felt on speeding away.
She stood watching me leave and waved,
a pathetic figure with grey hair,
understanding only that solitude beheads,
seeing in a dark cloud
a relentless presence
spouting words which still hung
in the heavy Toronto air,
"Four bastard children
with a man who married others!"

"I'm going to write about her!"
she had promised a year earlier
but was unable to give birth
to her mother.

Spurred on by ghosts and vacuums,
her triumph never quite filling
the shy chalice of a cup she held out
in a country she could not call her own
where loneliness dogged
till she cried out,
"I'd even welcome a cockroach
in my apartment—if it were alive!",
she returned to England,
to the brown soil of her Suffolk garden.

She sent me a postcard of an elm tree,
the trunk strong, in harmony with earth,
the branches reaching outward
flailing the empty sky.

AN ESCHER SPIRAL
for Samuel Beckett

Beak
le bec
Beckett.
Eagle: wide-ranging vision
that narrows
on burrowing blind moles
of truth. Peeling, paring,
cutting his master's blarney
down to the unbearable.
Yorick's skull ever-present.
But no 'alas.' No 'poor.'
No milksop *Weltschmerz*.

How to describe
in any but his words
him denying himself denying
that which is, was
him in a Dublin bathtub
letting the water run
hotter yes, yes hotter
still hotter oh
ohhhhh . . .
now denying all but
stirrings still
in himself descending
an Escher spiral
going neither down
nor up, just contracting
in spacetime.

He, holding the knife,
now focussing on his hands.

The peeling, paring hands
lying on the table before him
and on his hands,
his resting head
seen from behind
as if behind he stood
seeing himself rise
from his stool
and move
while the hour strikes
the clock paradox,
he the stationary observer
aging more quickly
than the observed moving
away.

MONSIEUR LUNETTES

Before his visits, the grownups sighed,
"Ah, pauvre homme!"
"And the gold injections?"
"Yes . . . But who knows how long . . . ?"
"Der arme Mann!"

We pictured gold rolling
through his veins
in small swift balls,
like mercury
from broken thermometers,

waited for it to prod his arms
or legs into sudden jerks
while he sat at the piano and played
Schumann.

Listening to him, the women wept.
"Why?" we whispered.
"He's dying. See the flame
in his eyes. Hear it in his music.
Poor man! Consumption."
"What's that?" we asked, frightened
though no wheedling Death Angel
gripped us by the throat
as in *Der Erlkönig*.

He rose, turned, we shrank
back, but craned to see
a flicker, felt cheated and relieved
by his thick-lensed glasses,
named him Monsieur Lunettes
and, quickly, once he had moved,
closed the lid
on the piano's dragon teeth.

KADDISH
for my mother

Memories tear at the fabric
of their weaving:
Chagall's village—
you the fiddler on the roof,
the Vitebsk milkmaid floating
above cupolas, the child
glimpsed in the womb—

you crossing Chagall's war-torn
Europe in his upside-down train,
scrambling off to find food,
water; the train hitting a mine;

your friends, his horizontal
pedestrians set on a collision course;

you singing—a glass-blower
shaping perfect sounds that reflect
colours, day and hour, your song
ending on a sob or laughter.

I close my eyes, strain
to hear another note,
you take my clenched hands,
straighten them
spanning octaves of pain,
joy, love, the backdrop
forever changing, fleeing
across borders,

you outrunning
the earth's rotation,
clinging with Chagall's seven
biblical fingers
to whatever sanity remained;

hearing the thrush's song
caught like a soul;   grieving
over an injured butterfly;

giving when you had nothing,
bearing sorrow too heavy
to bear,
unable to believe
but lighting Sabbath candles.

I hear another note, of sadness,
of destiny unfulfilled,
of what might have been . . .

laughing through tears, accepting
the cycle, new growth through old,
hiding the final note
of resignation,
your voice from the far side
of the world, "I love you".
Your last words, the telephone's click
a full stop marking the end.

Still I see you, leaping across tables
and, Chagall's Bella,
you float around me,
the little demon in your eyes
springing into mine.

UNMARKED DOORS

My father did his best,
covered his heartbeat
with a pocket watch,
checked it by every clock, at night
kept it near to rewind
should it stop,
though he had no illusions.

Stateless, he moved
through unmarked doors—
childhood, his only homeland—
a stranger trying to fit in,
the watch, a link, a rudder
steering him into accepted channels,
now, in this Dublin graveyard,
a stranger still.
I place reluctant pebbles on his grave.

Sunday morning bells fill
the soft Irish air, not for him,
under this angular stone slab
in rows of fearful symmetry.
No weathered curves. No flower
whose roots might split genealogies.

He remains a paradox of conformity
here where history is an epic
of rebellion yet days no more free-float
than beards, his one wish always
to have my mother at his side.
But she lies half-way across the world
in another symmetry.

He was a silent man,
his brief moments of happiness
before my time.

When I knew him
he stepped through happiness
as through a minefield, did not sing
like his brother who skipped
me along Sèvres streets
when I was four, teaching me a song,
     "On va bien s'amuser
       On va bien rigoler
       Avec les pom—pom
       Avec les pom—pom
       Aaah-vec les pompiers!"
My fun-loving uncle
who perished in Auschwitz.

I see my father
walking along Sandymount Strand
touching his hat to neighbours
barely glancing at them
for fear of intruding,
brooding if they looked
too hard at him. I want to slip
my arm through his and say:
It's alright. Really!

I want to stroke his smooth cheek
and ask: What colour
would the stubble be
if just once you didn't shave?

If I had the 78-record
of canned laughter he once bought
I would drop the needle on it
and cry. It was the only thing
that made him laugh.

THE BRANDING
for R.F.

His family had stayed in Paris,
even when the Germans came,
thought they were safe.
Mine had got out—just in time.

"You too have a plural voice,"
he said the day I was voiceless
and clambered round
on the twisted strands of his,
now and then sliding,
abruptly landing at this root or that,
now and then chafing
the invisible branding,
all of this filtered
through the slit
of the closet door
where he'd hidden for endless hours
or was it days?
fifty years before
—a ten-year old—
and emerged as from a womb
into a motherless world.

"A second birth, complete with crap"
he said. He had come out,
his skin intact,
the invisible branding
reaching ever deeper,
not thinking about souls
or where they had gone
but empty skins
of those he loved

—made into lampshades?
God!...
could not exist.

Walking on streets
as through a jungle
he learned survival

still teeters
on the edge of an abyss
no one sees
then pirouettes with words
wondering
about his mother
who had pushed him into the closet
when the boots pounded up the stairs
then carefully averted her eyes
as they marched her out.

Now, fifty years later,
in a light-hearted story
that flows easily from his hand
the heroine, without warning,
suddenly takes a job
in a factory
where lampshades are made

only the shadow of his clenched fist
marks the white page
—again the question overwhelms:

did his mother shade the light
on some official's desk?

TO A GERMAN FRIEND

Our eyes meet, suspicious
though it is long, long after
the event, even after the aftermath
—if there is such an after—
she, a daughter of the annihilator
I, a survivor.

The man who brought us together
stands between us, quietly confident
good sense would prevail,
Christian charity. Besides,
she was too young, had only been
a toddler then. And, after all,
no violence had touched me
. . . only those close to me.

Only later did she feel guilt
for the first time, she tells him,
balks at having to teach
that section of history to her class.
"Why?" I ask when he tells me,
"Why now if not before?"
"Because she was drawn to you."
"And if I fall short, will she
revert?" He makes no reply.
His silence says it is another
time, another place.

Is time not a continuum?
Are all places not one?

Again we meet.
She wants only my ear at first,
then, driven, seeks out my hidden face,
soon all of me.

Part and counterpart,
we eat ashes like bread,
wash them down with denial,
choke on doubt.

STARRY NIGHT
(Van Gogh)

Barely a touch of green
survives in cypress flames
towering above the village,
dwarfing the church spire,
burning higher
than the pincer-moon's
trapped shadow,
defying headstrong galaxies
—grasping vortices
in frenzied sky.

"Look," he pointed,
"mountains turn away,
the Milky Way pales
before sun-stars'
charging nipples.
Hear me, oh Lord!
See village doors shut
against a blighted world,
while lighted windows deny
overwhelming odds.
Hear me . . ."

SAINT MATTHEW PASSION
at Saint Joseph's Cathedral

No dove with olive leaf
this mighty bird,
pounding blood drawn
from vinegar-moistened
crucified flesh

breath of ecstasy
and devastation blown
into its nostrils

it soars
with powerful wingbeat
against stained glass

hangs trapped
under the roof

escapes
into night's chill
Adam's fall made manifest

then rises
toward distant Pluto
to wring tears from his ice heart.

On the corner
two prostitutes laugh.

WHIRL IS KING

PATTERN

Photons
infinitely moving
hurry, convey messages,
mediate, do all they can
and on the furthest edge
a tiny crystal of illusion
teeters.

Curious, this state of being
almost but not quite
perfectly ordered,
regular on a large scale
but not on the small,
the whole bathed in the fading glow
of a primeval burst
which fashioned every known feature
before the briefest fraction
of a second had elapsed
and lurks still
in seemingly empty fields.

PRESENCE

. . . but first? Awareness.
A seeping tide. Then a cadence
till unformed void, breathless,
melted into pliant arc,
a hollow acquiescence receiving
brunt of incubus—both mate
and progeny in one. Imagine
harmonics that defy all sound,
our seed inherent somewhere
in that early dust, some billion
years later finding again
—almost—the very first Moment:
in particle mouths
the quiver of musical strings,
that hunger, touch and join
then part again . . . in keeping
with all we know.

DANCE

To be Lucretius
and scry the atom's dance
in sunlit dust
or Saint Augustine and sense
World and Time
were born in single thrust

see them twined
like DNA—staggering
every whorl and gyre

and find in chaos
the comfort of recurrent patterns
—warted heartshapes

then draw a string
round this holistic womb. . . .

VAGUE PROMISES

How many flaring suns
daily stamp their seal on wax-red
skies of other-world horizons
while filaments of oxygen,
the spew of supernovae,
trail vague promises of life
seeded with doubt,
while protons
wallow in longevity
and, in the wings,
gravitational waves
pound upon consciousness?

Yes, Aristophanes,
Whirl is King.

SUBSTANCE

A chain-stitch in the cosmos,
appealing blue deflecting mind
from its real substance,
Halley's comet links
man's generations
—wisps of comprehension
in the multi-layered fabric
once, before the Beginning,
before Time or Word or Thought,
before Before, a Vacuum
solitary, black,
that flickered, tensioned
—the thread was spun

fragile,
in interstellar vacuums
particle pairs appear
snuff each other
before their existence impinges. . . .

MOTION

Age-old tribes, these galaxies
describe their psychedelic swirls
through pock-marked
space where black holes of hot
breath inhale what light
they catch—then blow
into some other universe?

And there does God appear
in mirror image?
Kant flip his imperative?
Observed change places
with observers
always hampered
by uncertainty, the counterpart
of any interaction?

LEGATO

Mozart phrases lift, catch light,
drift toward loose-webbed cloud
of molecules performing
on midnight skies, starlings
in migration training, till
tentacles of gravity ensnare,
cobble them tight into stars
then flick them spinning
their way through light years.

Ammonites, sightless Mesozoic
eyes, stare at other species'
rise, wobble and fall across
earth's ages
while invisible mass
obscurely fills the well of space
and swelling entropies
obey the rules.

DESTINIES

What plasma destinies
in magnetism's hands
—lineaments of longing
swayed and overruled
in the stir of cosmic vat!
Oh such febrile reaching out
in this expanding universe. . . .

Will many-fingered time
uncurl the smallest dimension
then suddenly retract
—a severed life-line?
Allow discrete finger-spirits
still to play and wander
in the dark of spatial wastelands?

INFINITY'S A FIGURE-EIGHT

The word is fleshed. The atom
split. The pit confirmed.
We're free to pick within
the loops. Magnetic moments
tiptoe among rubble.

Anaxagoras knew the sun
to be a a fiery pebble
but not that its existence
counts as an event in search
of its own meaning;
nor that events, brief candles
are the stuff of worlds.

LEAPS

Since Galileo's starry visions
pierced dark's canopy with ciphers,
thoughts have learned
to people atoms. In and outside
are the same. Past and present
will collide. Parity is just
reflection. An arsy-versy
tour de force.

Massless fields, geometry
bewitched, will bend.
Does truth have mass?
In malediction? Crystals prove
not all is curved
in this deep cartography
where every page is spectred
with a leap
to its own age's inquisition.

PRESTO

Singularities? . . .
They're tucked behind event
horizons. Out there
cosmic censorship enfolds
where time will stop
but not reverse. On earth
there's no such luck.
We're stuck
with a recurring past.

Tidiness above all things.
That's why from time to time
we pluck an unsuspecting second
out of space and, gloating,
ram it down our clockwork's throat.

But where light fails
fireflies in ten dimensions
tease till every quark
and lepton trembles.

COSINE

Upstairs, in Trinity's library
Byron, redeemed, sits enthroned
his dark dream not all a dream.

Beneath Nevile's pillars
bats flit from black to black;
must wonder what we're at where
Newton paced, Leibnitz frowned
and Schrödinger's cat
in half-life lurks, sniffs
at flavoured particles,
at numbers with soul that sigh
Dante's *Inferno*; at hands
once the limbed fins of lungfish
scribbling progress on sand,
now cupping microchips
that would gorge
on earth's clouded face.
Not without trace. Mass is
a constant and even cold stars
with no hint of heart, pulsate

while Shelley, with a glint,
is the Universe's eye.

NORTHERN JOURNEY

AUYUITTUQ
Northwest Territories

We felt the Ice Age linger
knew it could start again
under weak suns

saw the white-lipped horizon
of a world
that had never been young

spoke a language
not of sound
but great arcs

then boreal cotton seduced
with fluffy softness
purple saxifrage kindled
ice crystals and we breathed
warm guilt into cold air
till the illusion became complete
and self-sustaining

forgetting Goddess Earth
was bedded here by Odin
who still roars mockery
across the glaciers

here, where the narwhal turns
a simple tooth into a sword
and the loon bursts into mad laughter.

Even the ice groans.

WINTER SKY
Alberta

We laid offerings of silence
at one another's feet
then stumbled over.them
your eyes desperate
eloquent prisoners
and the moon
a forbidden apple
tasted and hurled back
to the black tree of night
bereft of birds
stretching to infinity
hung with crowns
of glinting thorns.

All at once the arctic wind
stopped time
careful not to ruffle
wafting wings
or quench flaming feet
and allowed the Aurora
to dance.

DELTA
Northern Manitoba

The barest touch of hands
or pressure of elbows
and instantly we had the taste
of forest fires in our throats
as do the whistling swans
spurred on to this oasis
where they pluck
preludial sky-strings
and only then descend
in majestic garlands.

We saw smoke rise,
felt but did not see the raging
flames envelop stoic spruce,
their every needle erect
till the last crumbling moment,
the same moment that liberates
the jack pine cone
after years of waiting
for chastity to melt
in a blaze so it can open
at last
and lick dry lips.

In flayed fields
under unmelting skies,
sand-coloured tumbleweed
flung itself
into a delirious fertility romp.

KLUANE GLACIERS
Yukon Territory

Some crawl to their death
others gallop
—surging waves
across arid valleys.

You came down standing tall.

But all who descend
abandon hope

like Dante's Ugolino
they pass over their progeny
unable to feed on them
with his choked voice
they cry their penitence
but no confessor hears them

victims, not of the devil
but of their passions,
of the spirit within,
hell on earth, life
an incessant dying,
stretching the present
to infinity,
pausing at the apex
of existence—the split second
after the last step of the climb
spelling finality

. . . and resurrection.

MOUNT ST. HELENS
Washington State

Unuttered

inner hell and heavens
contained in torment

the dark throb
held back under glacial ice

in one unguarded instant
exploded all reasoning
defied all will
gave way to earth-shaking sobs
you could no longer hear
bled molten rock
you could no longer see
and no one else understood.

I watched the clouds cathedral
and bowed my head.

On northern prairies
the whisper of grey ash

the only word.

Note on the Author

Born in Frankfurt of Russo-Polish parents, Inge Israel spent her childhood mostly in France and her adolescence in Dublin. In Canada since 1958, she makes her permanent home in Edmonton. Fluent in four languages, she still travels widely.

Inge Israel has written extensively for radio; her work has been broadcast on the BBC and the CBC French and English Networks.

UNMARKED DOORS is her fifth book of poetry, her second in English.